DAFT YORKSHIRE FAIRY TALES

... once upon a time ...

Daft Yorkshire Fairy Tales

written by
Ian McMillan

illustrated by
Tony Husband

Dalesman

First published in 2012 by Dalesman
an imprint of
Country Publications Ltd
The Water Mill, Broughton Hall
Skipton, North Yorkshire BD23 3AG
www.dalesman.co.uk

Text © Ian McMillan 2012
Cartoons © Tony Husband 2012

ISBN 978-1-85568-310-5

Typeset in Stone Informal.

Printed in China by Latitude Press Ltd.

Contents

How to Write a Yorkshire Fairy Tale

by
Professor Walt Blenkinsop
Department of Folklore, Cleckheaton University

A number of my students have asked me, when they encounter me in the many bars that are dotted round the university like sheep on a Dales hillside, what are the main ingredients of a successful Yorkshire Fairy Tale, and what makes a Yorkshire Fairy Tale distinct from any other kind of Fairy Tale?

I myself have given the matter much thought when I frequent the said bars, and have prepared a definitive list of a few of the characteristics of a Yorkshire Fairy Tale so that my students and members of the public can attempt to create their own.

The beginning of the Fairy Tale must grab the reader's or listener's attention. There is simply no point in beginning on a rambling description of, say, a castle. The Yorkshire reader will grow bored. There is also no point in starting the tale with a list of exhortations and what are known in the tale-telling trade as 'come hithers'. So, in other words, it is useless to say:

"It wasn't in my time, and it wasn't in your time, it was in a time far away in a land on the other side over forever."

The Yorkshire reader will be snoring gently by this point. Much better to say:

"SITHI! LISSEN!"

This will get their attention.

Do not give your characters outlandish Fairy Story names like Rapunzel or Little Red Riding Hood. Seth or Betsy will do.

Think about your audience and their expectations. Yorkshire women would rather go on a night out with the lasses than go to a ball wearing glass slippers. Be warned.

Yorkshire readers like to read about people eating and things being eaten, so a Yorkshire reader would be happy if Goldilocks not only

ate the Three Bears' porridge but also their haslet, egg sandwiches, savoury duck and black pudding as well.

Yorkshire readers are, on the whole, realists. So rather than having Jack climb the Beanstalk to get to where the giant lives, it would be better if he caught a number 32 bus, and it would be much easier for the Yorkshire reader to comprehend the Three Billy Goats Gruff if the goats didn't actually talk. Bleating is acceptable.

Yorkshire readers of Fairy Tales like specific place names, so rather than Hansel and Gretel getting lost in the woods, they should get lost in Tong.

Follow these simple rules and your Fairy Tales will last forever.

Who's buying?

George Grimshaw's Impassioned Speech to His Brothers Who Are, as Usual, Taking No Notice

So, did you read that book? The one I got for yer? That book: *Grimm's Fairy Tales*. Yes, that one. Well, didn't anything strike yer? Didn't it? Well, let me tell yer: that book's a bestseller! Everybody buys it.

I bet them Grimm lads are sitting on a beach somewhere! I bet they're drinking a drink with a brolly in! I bet lasses in swimming costumes are fluttering their eyelashes at 'em!

What's that got to with us? I'll tell yer! See their name: Grimm. See our name: Grimshaw. Here's a thing: why don't we have a go at making a book of them theer fairy tales. It can't be hard can it? Think about it, boys: that beach; them drinks; them lasses.

How do you mean, we can't think of any? We can! I'm telling yer we can! It's easy. Er... The Three Billy Goats Mardy. How's that? The Pie Maker of Hamelin! The Lion, the Witch and the Self-assemble Bedroom Unit! See! It's easy.

You two think of one. Go on, between yer. Don't let me do all the work! Go on, get thinking.

How do yer mean Puss in Boots? That exists already! The idea is yer've got ter think of a new 'un! Puss in Clogs or summat. No, not Goldilocks and the Three Bears! There's already one called that. Watch my lips: There's. Already. One. Called. That.

Go on, think of a new 'un!

Grimshaw's Fairy Tales! We'll be rich! Rich! I'm waiting. Take yer time. Take yer time...

Ten Green Bottles
Hanging from Uncle Ted

Ten green bottles hanging from Uncle Ted
(repeat until exhausted)
And if one green bottle should fall from Uncle Ted
He'll just sup the other nine bottles instead!

Nine green bottles hanging from Uncle Ted
(repeat until collapse occurs)
And if one green bottle should fall from Uncle Ted
It doesn't make no odds 'cos he's got loads more in
his shed!

Eight green bottles hanging from Uncle Ted
(repeat until stupefied)
And if one green bottle should fall from Uncle Ted
He'd just go and borrow one from daft old Cousin Fred!

Seven green bottles hanging from Uncle Ted
(repeat until fossilised)
And if one green bottle should fall from Uncle Ted
He'd just grab another one from under Auntie's bed!

Six green bottles hanging from Uncle Ted
(repeat until line has no meaning)
And if one green bottle should fall from Uncle Ted
And fall onto his foot — good job his toecaps are
    pure lead!

Five green bottles hanging from Uncle Ted
(repeat until life has no meaning)
And if one green bottle should fall from Uncle Ted
He'd moan and shout real loud until his face was
    crimson red!

Four green bottles hanging from Uncle Ted
*(repeat until your face seems to be stuck in a Yorkshire
version of a rictus)*
And if one green bottle should fall from Uncle Ted
He'd scout round till he found it with his trusty
    A-to-Z!

TEN GREEN BOTTLES

Three green bottles hanging from Uncle Ted
*(repeat until you feel wearier than the weariest thing in
    the known Universe)*
And if one green bottle should fall from Uncle Ted
He'd turn the colour of a slice of truly mouldy bread!

Two green bottles hanging from Uncle Ted
(repeat until you're sucked into a black hole of nothingness)
And if one green bottle should fall from Uncle Ted
He'll follow the bottle from the place the bottle's rolled
    and fled!

One green bottle hanging from Uncle Fred
(repeat until … repeat until … zzzz … zzzzz)
And if one green bottle should fall from Uncle Fred
You'll wish you were in Cleethorpes or sunbathing
    by the Med!

No green bottles hanging from Uncle Fred
(repeat as often as you flipping like. I'm going to the pub!)
And if one green bottle should fall from Uncle Fred
That would be a physical impossibility because
    there were no bottles left or haven't you been
    listening to anything I've said?

There Was an Old Woman
Who Lived in a Curd Tart

There was an old Yorkshirewoman who lived
    in a curd tart
She had a bad heart
Through eating curd tart.
She ate through the curd tart walls
And she ate through the curd tart floors
And she ate through the curd tart ceilings
And she ate through the curd tart doors
And then she was homeless
And fat
And had a bad heart
And really didn't
Know
What
To
Do!

Why the Enormous Yorkshire Turnip Never Got Pulled Up

There was once an enormous turnip growing in the garden of Old Ted Micklethwaite at the far end of the main street. One day he said to his wife

"Eee, wife, I fancy some turnip for me dinner!"

and his wife said

"So do I!"

which was the longest conversation they'd had since 1983.

So Ted went into the garden and tried to pull the turnip up. He pulled and pulled but it wouldn't budge. So he said to his wife

"Here, wife, can you help me pull up this enormous turnip and then we'll have some turnip for us dinner?"

and she said

"No"

because she was an archetypal miserable and grumpy Yorkshire woman.

So Ted went into the garden where his five kids were playing and said

"Here, kids, can you help me pull up this enormous turnip and then we'll have some turnip for us dinner?"

And the kids said

"No"

because they were archetypal miserable and grumpy Yorkshire children.

So Ted met a dog and asked the dog and the dog said

"No"

because it was an archetypal miserable and grumpy Yorkshire dog.

And the same happened to Ted when he asked a cat, a sheep, a pig, a cow and a horse.

So Ted went and looked at the turnip.

"I'm sorry I can't pull yer up," he said, his voice cracking at the edges with emotion, "but none of the archetypal miserable and grumpy

Yorkshire people and animals round here will help me."

And the turnip replied

"Well, I don't want to be pulled up anyway because I'm an archetypal miserable and grumpy Yorkshire turnip!"

Moral: If you want a turnip, go to Shropshire.

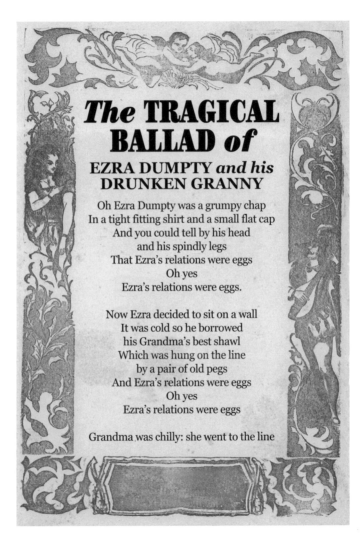

The TRAGICAL BALLAD *of*

EZRA DUMPTY *and his* DRUNKEN GRANNY

Oh Ezra Dumpty was a grumpy chap
In a tight fitting shirt and a small flat cap
And you could tell by his head
and his spindly legs
That Ezra's relations were eggs
Oh yes
Ezra's relations were eggs.

Now Ezra decided to sit on a wall
It was cold so he borrowed
his Grandma's best shawl
Which was hung on the line
by a pair of old pegs
And Ezra's relations were eggs
Oh yes
Ezra's relations were eggs

Grandma was chilly: she went to the line

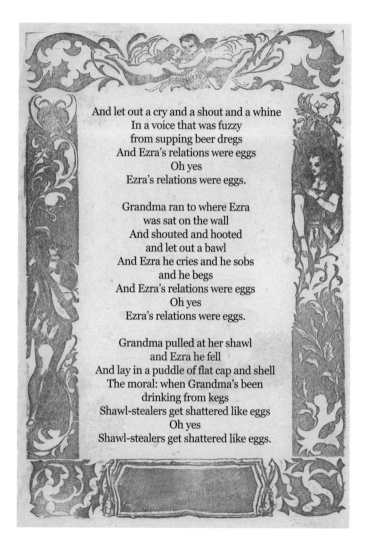

And let out a cry and a shout and a whine
In a voice that was fuzzy
from supping beer dregs
And Ezra's relations were eggs
Oh yes
Ezra's relations were eggs.

Grandma ran to where Ezra
was sat on the wall
And shouted and hooted
and let out a bawl
And Ezra he cries and he sobs
and he begs
And Ezra's relations were eggs
Oh yes
Ezra's relations were eggs.

Grandma pulled at her shawl
and Ezra he fell
And lay in a puddle of flat cap and shell
The moral: when Grandma's been
drinking from kegs
Shawl-stealers get shattered like eggs
Oh yes
Shawl-stealers get shattered like eggs.

The Goose that Laid
the Golden Eggs

John By-eck was known throughout the dale as a man who was good with his hands but not so good with his brains.

"Strong in t' arm and thick in t' head," he used to say of himself, proudly, to anyone who would listen.

He got by as a farmer but the work was hard and the profits were low. Then one day a goose wandered into the farmyard, and John was overjoyed. He liked goose eggs, and he knew that any goose eggs he couldn't eat himself, he could sell.

The next day he sat by the goose and waited patiently for her to lay; suddenly she produced a huge egg of the purest gold that gleamed in the Sun.

John picked it up and ran into the house with it. He tried to crack it over the frying pan but nothing happened, except that after several attempts the frying pan was permanently bent and buckled out of shape. He put it in a pan of boiling water and boiled it for twelve minutes but he still couldn't get into the egg.

He went outside; the goose was still laying and six gleaming golden eggs rolled around the farmyard. John took them into the house and tried to make an omelette but no matter how hard he tried, he couldn't crack any of the eggs.

So he took the eggs to the top of his track and put them by the main road in a basket with a sign that said

GOOSE EGGS FOR SALE
WARNING: THE SHELL IS DISCOLOURED
AND EXTREMELY TOUGH

John's neighbours couldn't believe their eyes and they bought the eggs by the dozen. And the goose kept laying the golden eggs and the neighbours kept buying them.

And this all started to happen many years ago and it's still happening. If you go up the dale today you can find the basket at the end of the farm track. You have to look quite hard, though; the palaces and fancy cars of the neighbours almost obscure it from view.

Jack Sprat
The Yorkshire Years

Jack Sprat could eat no tripe
His wife could eat no parkin
His favourite pyjamas had a narrow stripe
His sink it had a shark in.

Humpty Dumpty

*retold in incomprehensible
Yorkshire dialect*

Seez, this kid oo looked a bit like a free-ranger, one o' them tha gets frum a proper butchers not wun o' thi supermarket puffan-waffum wo' sat on a wall and wind wo' blowing fair to rip this clarts off 'n' mek thi eez watter.

And does tha know what? He tummels off. Reyt off. Hits flooar wi' a reyt bang and if me old mam 'ud have been theer she'd 'a' sharted:

"Send 'em dahn David!"

Like she used to when it thundered and leetened.

'E sat theer in smithers and smithereens and smithereenettes and so I gorron t' blower and

sent fo' t' king's osses and t' kings blokes and duz tha know what? They woh flummoxed! They who as much uiss as a sausij in a Lancashire wardrooab.

And that's it. E's still theer if tha wants to 'ave a gawp.

Goldilocks Goes to a Yorkshire Barber

"Can you do something with this, old love?
It's tangled and won't stay in place.
It feels like a wig that's been dropped from above
And it lolls down all over my face."

Geoff Utley, gents' barber. Trim or a good trim.
He's listening.

"I'm off for a walk in the woods after dinner,
Exercise: good for the heart.
But snipping my locks will make me feel thinner
And, as they say, it's a start."

Geoff Utley, gents' barber. Trim or a good trim.
He's got a shop full.

"They tell me there's bears in the heart of the
    woods
But I don't believe that, oh no.
They got washed away in those terrible floods
They had all those long years ago."

Geoff Utley, gents' barber. Trim or a good trim.
Had the Big Bad Wolf in last week.

"I'm on a diet and all. Just lettuce and things.
I'm aiming to lose fifteen stone.
So when you've cut my hair and I've took off
    my rings
I'll be loose skin and sinew and bone."

Geoff Utley, gents' barber. Trim or a good trim.
The Three Bears are regulars. They're not flooded out.

"I don't really miss chips, I can live without steak,
Don't want pizza or pork luncheon meat.
But a life without porridge would make my heart
    break:
It fulfils me, makes my life complete."

Geoff Utley, gents' barber. Trim or a good trim.
The bears have been in earlier. Gone home to make
* porridge.*

"Thanks, Barber, that's better! I'm lighter already.
Now I'll go for that stroll, get me fit.
I'll not go too fast, I'll just take it steady,
Make my heart race the tiniest bit."

Geoff Utley, gents' barber. Trim or a good trim.
Should he tell her there's porridge at the bears' place?
No. Why spoil a good story?

Jack and the Beans Talk

Jack lived with his mam in a little cottage at the edge of the village of East Westerton, near the crossroads. This is relevant because at the other side of the crossroads, for many years, was the East Westerton Bean Factory which made, according to many locals (and one or two people from West Easterton too), the best baked beans in the land.

Jack and his mam were content with their lives; he went to the local school under the strict but kindly tutelage of Mrs Ferris, and she worked as a chimney sweep and frogherd for Lord Tootal at the Big House, East Westerton Hall.

One day at the start of a new term Mrs Ferris announced in a kindly but strict way that everyone in the class had to prepare a little speech that would deliver to the rest of the class.

"Make it about something interesting," she said, "so that the rest of us aren't bored to death!"

Jack was interested in beans; he loved the taste of them, the smell of them (and the smell of the factory on Bean Baking Mornings) and the sight of them on the plate, so it was obvious what he would wax lyrical on when it was his turn. And his turn came soon enough!

It was a Tuesday morning, and the Sun shone, glinting on the tall chimneys of the Baked Bean Factory. Mrs Ferris invited Jack to the front. He unfolded several large sheets of paper and began to talk about beans.

And he talked and talked. And he carried on talking. He talked about the physical properties of beans, the mental and spiritual stimulation they give to the chewer, the history of the baked bean, the way that the baked bean can be made into sculptures of small woodland animals and much, much more.

For the first hour his fellow pupils and Mrs Ferris were interested. After three hours their eyes began to droop and they yawned jaw-cracking yawns. Jack carried on, as parents came and took their children home and Mrs Ferris applied for a new job in Harrogate, got it and left the school.

People say there was something in the air around the Baked Bean Factory that had otherworldly properties that would seize you if you were the right kind of person. Well, Jack must have been that kind of person.

He's still there, all those years later, still talking about beans. He's middle-aged now and the school has been closed for many years but Jack's still standing in the old classroom talking about beans. His mother visits him every day, changes his clothes, feeds him when he takes a breath. But even as he's chewing he carries on his bean-monologue.

Go and visit him if you like. The old school's right in the middle of East Westerton. You can't miss it. If you get to South Northerton you've gone too far.

I Saw Three Ships Come Sailing By, Tha Knaws

I saw three ships come sailing by
Come sailing by
Come sailing by
I saw three ships come sailing by
On Christmas Day in the morning

And that was odd 'cos I live inland
I live inland
I live inland
And that was odd 'cos I live inland
In Barnsley in South Yorkshire

I said to my wife "I saw three ships
Did you see t' ships?
Did you see t' ships?"
I said to my wife "Did you see t' ships?"
And she said to me "You're sackless!"

My wife then said "That cheese was off!
That cheese was off!
That cheese was off!"
My wife then said "That cheese was off
That you had yesterday morning!"

Hallucinating ships I was
Ships I was
Ships I was
Hallucinating ships I was
So let this be a warning:

Never eat ancient Wensleydale
Wensleydale
Wensleydale
Never eat ancient Wensleydale
Or you'll see ships where there are none!

Fee Fi Fo Fum

Fee Fi Fo Fum
I smell the blood of a Yorkshireman
Be he alive or be he dead
He always eats Yorkshire Puddings
between two slices of bread!

A Yorkshire Humpty Dumpty

Yorkshire Humpty Dumpty sat on a wall
Yorkshire Humpty Dumpty had a great fall

Yorkshire Humpty Dumpty's mam came out
and said
I told you not to sit on that wall you daft
ha'porth!'

Yorkshire Humpty Dumpty's dad came out and
said
"Tha's landed on me rhubarb and flattened it!"

Yorkshire Humpty Dumpty's brother came out
and said
"You're in trouble now! At least it's you this
time and not me!"

Yorkshire Humpty Dumpty's sister came out
and said
"I didn't really mean that you should sit on
the wall! I was only joking!"

Yorkshire Humpty Dumpty said
"I wish I'd never climbed on the flaming
wall! I've got a reyt headache an' all!"

Let's leave them there shall we, readers,
bickering gently in the breeze...

Ralph Hunshelf, Ralph Hunshelf, Let Down Your Hair

There once was a man in Lofthouse called Ralph Hunshelf who, as a younger chap-about-Lofthouse, had a full head of thick black hair. As he got older he followed the tradition of all the other males in his family and began to go bald, so that by the time he was twenty-six he had had to resort to the combover, which in his case looked like a child's scribble on a 50-watt light bulb.

Ralph was embarrassed about his combover and the way it flailed in the wind, almost lassooing unsuspecting nesting birds, and so he gradually withdrew from society, or what passes for society in Lofthouse*, by retreating to the upper floor of his four-storey house.

*I'm joking

41

His childhood sweetheart Joyce had emigrated to Lancashire when she and Ralph were both ten and it had broken both their hearts. When Joyce and her family returned, the language barrier having proved too much, Joyce was eager to get back in touch with Ralph and was disappointed to find he had become a combover-induced recluse. She was determined that four storeys and the lack of a quiff wouldn't put her off, though and one night she stood below Ralph's window shouting

Ralph Hunshelf, Ralph Hunshelf,
Let down your hair
So that I may climb up it
And give you a big sloppy kiss!

After some initial reluctance, Ralph unrolled his combover and let it down to the ground so that Joyce could climb up it. Unfortunately love was to be thwarted when the strand of hair broke when Joyce was halfway up and she fell into the canal.

Moral: Always wear a lifejacket when dating a man with a combover.

Where There's Mick There's Brass

Mick Mason was an ordinary boy who lived with his mam and dad in a terraced house in Huddersfield; one morning he woke up and he said to his mam:

"Mam, Mam, me fingers are tingling,

What shall I do, mam,

What shall I do?"

And she told him not to be daft and that he'd probably slept in a funny position. So Mick went to his dad and said:

"Dad, Dad, me fingers are tingling,

What shall I do, Dad,

What shall I do?"

And his dad told him to ask his mam, and this would have gone on a long time, possibly even until bedtime, but then a remarkable thing happened: Mick felt hungry after all that rhythmic repetition, so he reached out for an apple in the fruit bowl on the sideboard and when he grabbed it, it turned to brass instantly. Foolishly, Mick tried to bite it and broke a tooth. He then picked up all the other fruit in the bowl and that turned to brass, too.

He shouted to his mam and dad:

"Mam and Dad, Mam and Dad,

I've got strange brassy powers,

What shall I do?

What shall I do?"

And his dad ran into the room clutching his cup of tea and Mick reached out and touched the cup and it turned to brass; Mick's dad looked at it dumbfounded. Mick's mam ran into the room and Mick touched her pinny and it turned to brass.

Mick's dad looked confused but Mick's mam shouted in triumph, her voice a little strangled because the brass pinny was pretty heavy.

"Have you seen the price of brass! It's gone through the roof recently! We're going to be rich!"

And she ran forward and embraced her husband and Mick, and they all danced round the room holding on to each other.

And that was their first mistake.

And their last.

You can pay to see them now, in their house which is now a museum to their folly. They look like a sculpture, a lovely gleaming brass sculpture.

Don't get too close, though.

Sing a Grim Song of Yorkshire

Sing a song of Yorkshire

A pocket full of grimness

Four and twenty flat caps

Baked in a grimness pie

When the pie was opened, grimly,

The caps began to fly, grimly, through the grim Yorkshire air because the pie was so hot it had created a grim vacuum.

Wasn't that a grim and yet typically Yorkshire thing to do, to bake flat caps in a pie because, although they have almost no nutritional value, they're cheaper than blackbirds this week?

Jack and t' Bean Tins

Once upon a time there was a lad called Jack who lived with his mam in a terraced house somewhere in Yorkshire. I realise that narrows it down a bit, but there you go.

Jack's dad had left years before, saying he was just popping out to the shop for some Yorkshire Mixtures and an evening paper but he never came back. And he didn't even like Yorkshire Mixtures.

So Jack's mam brought Jack up on her own; she held down three jobs, cleaning at the Clog Factory, pulling barges through Glassborough Tunnel and taking Squire Fitzwilliam's dogs for walks.

One winter, though, things got really tough; the Clog Factory went on short time due to the

West Yorkshire Welly Fad, she was replaced on the barge-pulling by Dobbin, and three of the squire's dogs were sold to pay death duties on the fourth.

It was a Thursday evening and there was nothing in the cupboard for Jack and his mam's tea. Nothing that is except a tin of baked beans. Value baked beans. Value baked beans way past their munch-by date. The choice was stark: either eat the beans or try to sell them to Mrs Dean next door who was always partial to a tin of beans, even those bought fifteen years before. Then use the money to buy fresher beans.

Jack was despatched next door, where he found Mrs Dean looking into her own bare cupboard. She turned to him with a face like a half-melted candle.

"Nowt," she said, a tolling bell of a voice. "Well, nearly nowt…"

She reached into the depths of the cupboard and pulled out a tiny tin of beans, no bigger than a thimble. Jack held out his tin of beans, which looked huge in comparison.

"Do you want to buy these beans, Mrs Dean?" he said.

"I've no dosh but I'll swap them for this tin of Magic Beans," she said, her voice cracking with age and gin.

Jack wasn't very clever or handsome but he was certainly gullible, and his face glowed with excitement.

"If you put this tin in the middle of your yard and say 'BeanyBeanyBean' it'll grow a tower of bean tins right up to the sky' said Mrs Dean, trying to smile, although it made her face hurt.

Jack gave her the tin of beans and ran home with the tiny tin. His mam, understandably, was really cross.

"She's diddled you!" she yelled, and flung the tin of beans into the yard.

Jack, sobbing like a cistern (as they used to say in Cleckheaton), ran into the yard and whispered 'BeanyBeanyBean' to the tin. Nothing happened. He whispered it again. 'BeanyBeanyBean'. He whispered it again. 'BeanyBeanyBean'.

Of course nothing happened. This is Yorkshire after all.

Yorkshire Counting Rhyme

One two
Buckle my clog

Three, four
Knock at the window and shout
    "Hey! Them's my parsnips!"

Five, six
Pick up sticks and chase them that's
    pinched yer parsnips.

Seven, eight
Lay them straight out with a couple
    of blows from the sticks

Nine, ten
A big fat apology when you realise it
    was just your brother and his mate
    bringing you some parsnips from
    their allotment...

The Ballad of
The Elvis and the Shoemaker

Friday nights you'd see him,
And Saturdays and all;
Colin doing Elvis at the Working Men's Club
Rolling his hips like a ball.

His quiff was sharp as a breadknife;
T' sneer was bent and true
There was only one thing he couldn't get right:
He hadn't any Blue Suede Shoes.

He made do with his dad's old pit boots;
They pinched his tiny feet
And they didn't give the right impression
When he Elvis'd down the street.

THE ELVIS AND THE SHOEMAKER

One night he passed a shoe shop
Late and t' shop were dark
And his quiff it quivered like a radar
And his Elvis voice mouthed "Hark …

I can hear somebody in t' cellar.
Somebody making shoes.
Let's see if they can do me some suede 'uns
In a Memphis shade of blue."

He peeped in the cellar window,
Saw a cobbler and his last
Churning shoes out quickly.
"By gum," said Colin, "he's fast!"

Colin climbed in the window,
Confronted the shoe shop man,
Said "I'm an Elvis impersonator
And do you think you can

Make me some shoes in a shade of blue
And suede please if you could?"
And the cobbler nodded a cobbler's nod
As though he understood.

The next day Colin went back to the shop
In his Elvis jumpsuit, white;
And when he saw what the shoemaker'd made
He hollered in delight:

Blue Suede Shoes size four no less,
Gleaming like blue suede gold,
And Colin put 'em on and they fitted like gloves
And Colin shouted "Sold!"

And ran from the shop down to the club
As the cobbler tried to say
"They're magic shoes — you'll never get 'em off"
But Colin was far away.

That was fifteen years ago
And Colin's never managed
To get those shoes off his poor feet
And his toes are permanently damaged.

And not only that, these magic shoes
Dance all day and night
And Colin/Elvis has never sat down
To his mates in the club's delight.

He gyrates like a whirlwind,
He leaps just like a pup.
There's one thing you can say about Colin:
He's really All Shook Up!

Hansel and Gretel

*an extract from an early, and later
discarded, draft*

…and Hansel and Gretel came through the woods to a clearing and there, shaded by the trees from the harsh Sun, was the most amazing house they'd ever seen. It was made entirely of Yorkshire pudding, with parkin for chimneys and the windows made of tripe and the door made of a huge curd tart.

"Well, I'll go to the foot of our stairs," said Hansel to Gretel. "This house looks terrible!"

"It does that, does it not," said Gretel to Hansel.

"Who the ummer would ever want a house like that?" said Hansel. "Now, if it was a house made of hotpot that would be a different thing altogether."

And Hansel and Gretel laughed and ran back home through the woods.

And the wicked witch sat in house and waited for someone to come so that she could eat them up. And nobody ever came. Because she was from Yorkshire, and the woods were in Lancashire.

By heck!

Prince Charming
Tries to Explain

I were nearly late to t' ball. Well, I'd got reading a book and I looked up and it were ten past by t' sundial and I knew I were late even though it weren't sunny. I got Eric to power t' cart up and we dashed round to t' Palace and t' ball were in full swing.

I'm not much o' a prince I know; I'm not that bothered about huntin' and dancin' and countin' me dosh. I'd rather read a good book. So anyway we got to t' ball and there's t' ugly sisters looking like a cross between two submarines and two piles of discarded orange peel and they wanted to dance wi' me but I said summat about needin' to get a drink and I scuttled away and I managed to keep 'em at bay.

Then I saw this lass and she were a reyt crackerjack, looked reyt nice in a nice frock and wi' her hair done and she were wearing these glass slippers like. I went red and I daren't say owt but then she come up to me and she asked me. I were amazed. That's modern lasses, I suppose.

Well, she danced reyt well and we got to chattin' and that and it turned out she liked books and all. We started talkin' about all the ones we'd read and, well, t' evening flew by. Then just as we were rattlin' away she suddenly looks up at t' sundial and she sharts

"Ah've got ter gu!"

and she runs off. And she runs that fast that one o' t' glass slippers slipped off of her foot.

So I figured that t' onny way to find who she was were to see who t' glass slipper fitted. So t' next day I organised a walk-past of all t' lasses who were at t' ball.

Them daft ugly sisters lumbered up but there were no way that sliopper would go any-where near their big tooaz, nivver mind their feet.

Then old Cinderella comes up and them ugly sisters laughed and I thought she weren't at t' ball but then I sort of recognised her even though she weren't dressed up and so I thought "well, I'll gie it a goa", and I lifted t' slipper towards her foot.

And then I dropped it an' it shattered into a million bits. And that were it. So I went back and read a book.

Two People at a Bus Stop Discuss Hansel and Gretel

Did you hear about that Hansel?
Aye.
And that Gretel?
Aye.
Nearly got their sens etten by a witch, didn't they?
That they did.
Their poor dad.
Should nivver have married that lass.
Nay.
Should have stuck to t' woodcuttin'.
Aye.
Shouldn't have joined that online dating agency.
What were it called again?
Wickedstepmothersforu.com

He should have been warned off by t' name.

What, Nancy?

No, I meant name on t' website.

Oh. Aye. Well, he were nivver t' brightest log in t' pile.

Since that accident wi' that bit of oak.

Aye.

Nose.

Eh?

It went up his nose, not in his eye.

Aye.

Nose, aye.

Good job they got away, though.

Aye, she were set to eyt 'em.

Just shows, dun't it?

What?

Eh?

What does it show?

Er … I dunno. I thowt these fairy tales were always supposed to show yer summat, though. Tell you summat about t' deeper meta-narrative.

What time's that bus due?

Humpty Dumpty

*rewritten to the the tune of
'On Ilkley Moor Baht 'At'*

verse 1:
Why are tha lyin' on the floor?
On the floor?
Looking all shattered and broken?
Why are tha lyin' on the floor
On the floor
Why are tha lyin' on the floor?

chorus:
Tha's fallen off the wall!
Tha's fallen off the wall!
Tha's fa...llen off the wall!

verse 2:
Tha should have been more careful, thee!
Looking all shattered and broken...

..Tha's fallen off the wall..
Tha's fallen off the wall...
TONIGHT LIVE...
1+2=3 YORKSHIREMEN

verse 3:
We're gunner 'ave to scrape thee up!
Looking all shattered and broken

verse 4:
We'll have to send for all t' King's men!
Looking all shattered and broken

verse 5:
We'll have to fetch his hosses too!
Looking all shattered and broken

verse 6:
Then we shall have a reyt good laugh!
Looking all shattered and broken

There Was an Old Yorkshirewoman who Lived in a Clog

There was an old Yorkshirewoman
     who lived in a clog
With her fat idle husband
     and a small spotty dog.
She said "Come here Cyril:
     your toenails need clipping",
Then sent him to bed
     without any dripping!

The Piped Pi-er of Halifax

The people of Halifax were very hungry, and what they were really hungry for were pies.

Any kind of pie: big pies, bigger pies, huge pies, massive pies, enormous pies, vast pies; meat pies, apple pies, plum pies, plum and apple pies, plum and apple and meat pies; thick crusts, thin crusts, soft crusts, dusty crusts.

Put it this way: they liked pies. Indeed the mayor of Halifax was trying to get an act passed in Parliament to rename the town Pie. Not Pietown or Pieville. Just Pie.

The main supplier of all the pies eaten in Halifax was Mick 'Meat' Mason, master butcher. He employed an army of crust-mixers, pie-artisans and gravy-brewers in his factory-cum-shop on the high street.

Making the pies wasn't much of a logistical problem but the distribution of them was. No matter how fast his vans and trucks went out, they couldn't deliver the goods fast enough to the pie-hungry folk of Halifax. They always wanted more.

Then Mick had a brilliant idea: he'd dig pipes (which he renamed pie-pes) from his factory-cum-shop to every house in the town so that the citizens could just take the end of the pie-pes and pop them into their mouths and eat the pies to their heart's content.

And that's why Mick 'Meat' Mason was forever known as the Piped Pi-er of Halifax!

Little Yorkshire Ridings Hood

(Why not play this game at home?)
(I'll tell you why: it takes up all your time!)

Little Yorkshire Ridings Hood (her real name was Beverley) lived in a cottage in the Woodlesthorpe at the edge of a Mirfield with her mother and father. One Deighton her mother said to her:

"Little Yorkshire Ridings Hood, can you go and take this basket of food to your Grandma in her cottage at the other end of the Woodlesthorpe?"

And the little girl did as she was told and went to her Grandma's cottage.

Well, the time ticked and Tockwithed by, and eventually, with a hop, a Skipton and a

Jump Little Yorkshire Ridings Hood arrived at Grandma's. It really was a lovely little cottage, with Rosedales round the door and some Chickenleys clucking in the garden. Little Yorkshire Ridings Hood knocked and went in. There was no sign of Grandma, so Little Yorkshire Ridings Hood began to climb the stairs.

Little Yorkshire Ridings Hood had no idea that, earlier that Deighton, the Big Bad WHullf had got into the cottage and eaten Grandma up, and a couple of her Chickenleys for good measure as well as her dog, the one called Pontefract.*

The Big Bad WHullf was tucked up in Grandma's Cottingham (or is that a Cottingley?) and Little Yorkshire Ridings Hood could only partially see her face under her big bonnet.

"My, what big Earswick you've got, Grandma!" said Little Yorkshire Ridings Hood.

"All the better to HEarswick you with, my old Muker!" said the Big Bad WHullf.

"My, what big eyes you've got, Grandma!" said Little Yorkshire Ridings Hood.

well, how else am I going to get it in?

"All the better to see you with, my old Muker!" said the big bad WHullf.

"And what big TReeth you've got, Grandma!" said Little Yorkshire Ridings Hood.

"All the better to eat you with, my old Muker!" said the Big Bad Wolf.

"Oh no you're Notton! Oh no you're Knottingley!" said Little Yorkshire Ridings Hood, and ran away as fast as she possibly Cudworth.

Old King Clog

Old King Clog
Was a merry old dog
And a merry old dog was he.
He called for his tripe
And he called for his brawn
And he called for his whippets three!

'The Bogey Man will Get You'
some Yorkshire variations on the phrase

Old Steve the Dusty Boy
is Hiding Behind the Stool
(Grassington)

Nellie's Bringing Her Moppy Mop
if You Don't go to Sleep!
(Howden)

The Bin Lid Lads
are Blowing Their Trumpets
and They can't Hear Themselves Play
(Idle)

The Horse with No Legs or Head
is Rolling This Way
(Catterick)

The Owl Of Destiny
Has Looked at His Map
(*Leyburn*)

Fat Ronald's Wheezing:
Can you Hear Him?
(*Bawtry*)

Snow White and the Cantankerous Old Yorkshire Mirror

So Snow White went to the cantankerous old Yorkshire mirror and said

"Mirror, mirror, on the wall

Who is the fairest of them all?"

And the cantankerous old Yorkshire mirror said

"Tha what? I can't hear thi! Tha'll have to speyk up!"

And Snow White got closer to the cantankerous old Yorkshire mirror and said, in a voice that was loud and clear,

"Mirror, mirror on the wall

Who is the fairest of them all?"

And the old Yorkshire mirror said

"I can't answer that 'cos that's a question of them theer aesthetics. I'm only equipped to deal wi' factual stuff!"

And Snow White said

"Well, factually, am I fairer than the Wicked Witch?"

And the old Yorkshire mirror said

"Again, I can't give thi an answer to that 'cos it's not specific. Now, if tha'd asked if tha were taller than t' Wicked Witch or thinner, then I could have answered thi, but in fairness, unless tha talking in t' sense o' hair colour and I suspect tha not, that is a subjective judgement which I'm not prepared to gi'."

So Snow White reached into her bag and pulled something out.

"Mirror, mirror, on the wall

Can you tell me, factually,

What I'm holding in my hand?"

And the cantankerous old Yorkshire mirror said

"Now yer talking. That's, factually, a giant sledgehammer."

And Snow White said

"And, mirror, mirror, on the wall,

Can you tell me what I'm going to do with it?"

And the cantankerous old Yorkshire mirror said

"Aye, that I can...no...no...AAAARGH!"

Moral: Never argue with a fairytale character when she's holding a giant sledgehammer.

The Yorkshire Wind Blows

The Yorkshire wind blows
And we shall have snow
And what will old Alan do then,
   poor kid?
He'll sit in his van
And say "I'll not get a tan
If I spend all my winters in Brid!"*

*other, non-rhyming, Yorkshire seaside resorts are available

Local Man Held

"Just Wanted Change from Rabbit" – Claim

Norman Wetwang was today cautioned by Slatby Police after being arrested for causing a breach of the peace outside the home of butcher's daughter Rapunzel Woodend of High Street, Slatby.

Wetwang (48), a fettler's assistant at the local flannel mill, was reported to the authorities late on Tuesday evening.

"I saw him standing outside the butcher's, shouting up to the flat where the Woodends live," said neighbour Eileen Thomas (age undisclosed but not an hour less than 65). "He appeared to be shouting 'Rapunzel, Rapunzel, let down your hair' which doesn't make any sense as she's had it in a pageboy bob for years."

Pageboy Bob was unable to comment, being on a family holiday in Eastgrime Bay.

According to Mrs Thomas, Rapunzel Woodend then "stuck her head out of the window and shouted 'Get home you daft ha'porth!'", to which Norman replied "But I'm fed up with rabbit; I'll be looking like a rabbit soon", to which Rapunzel shouted "Who's that talking? It looks and sounds just like a rabbit!".

The police force then arrived and bundled the offender into the back of the police van and took him to Slatby Police station where Norman contended that he was simply asking Rapunzel to let down her hare because he wanted to jug it, having lived off rabbit pie for the last three weeks. He also said that he was shouting because after years in the flannel mill he was deaf and that he didn't know how late it was because he'd loaned his fob watch to their Eric because he was going to the Tripe Dance.

The case continues.

NER NER

Goldilocks and the
Three Awkward Yorkshire Bears

The Three Awkward Yorkshire Bears were out on a walk while their porridge cooled. Goldilocks nipped into their house for a look round, ignoring the note pinned to the door that said

THA'RE ONLY WELCOME
IF THA'RE AWKWARD

She sat on each of the Three Awkward Yorkshire Bears' chairs. Daddy Awkward's was too flipping hard as well as being awkward; Mummy Awkward's was too flipping soft as well as being awkward; but Babby Awkward's was just awkward enough. At least it was for about a minute, then it shattered under Goldilocks's weight.

Goldilocks then tried the porridge. Daddy

Awkward's was too saltily awkward; Mummy Awkward's was too sweetly awkward; but Babby Awkward's was just awkward enough.

After she'd eaten all the porridge, Goldilocks began to feel sleepy. She tried to lie down on Daddy Awkward's bed, but it was full of awkward lumps and bumps; she tried to lie down on Mummy Awkward's bed, but it was full of awkward valleys and slippages; so she tried to lie down on Babby Awkward's bed, and it was just awkward enough. So Goldilocks fell asleep.

Suddenly the Three Awkward Yorkshire Bears came home.

"This is awkward," said Daddy Awkward. "It looks like somebody's been in the house; the door's at an awkward angle."

"Well, it is," said Mummy Awkward, awkwardly, "but I quite like it."

"Somebody's been sitting in our chairs," Babby Awkward shouted, "and mine's all smashed!"

"Well, you always said you didn't like it," said Mummy Awkward, awkwardly.

"Somebody's been eating our porridge," said Daddy Awkward, "and I'm really pleased because I never liked porridge anyway."

The other two agreed, just to be awkward, although Mummy Bear did confess that six bowls of porridge one after the other made her feel a bit, well, awkward.

Then Babby Awkward found Goldilocks asleep in his bed and, when he'd told his Mummy and Daddy, they just left her there and moved to the next town. Just to be awkward, you understand.

The Three Little Pigs
and the Wolf That Got it Wrong

I got this story from Denise Waterton from Durkar who, as you'll hear, got it from someone else ...

This was a tale my Grandad Horace used to tell when we went to visit him. He'd sit on one end of the settee and all us kids would crowd round the other end and he'd say

"You all know the tale of the three little pigs and the wolf that blew their houses down?"

and we'd say

"Yes Granddad, we do"

and he'd say

"And you know how he blew down the house made of straw and the house made of sticks without too much trouble?"

And we'd say
"Yes, Granddad"
and there were six of us kids so it made quite
a row.

And he'd say

"And do you know why the Big Bad Wolf couldn't blow the house of bricks down?"

and we'd say

"No, Granddad"

even though we really knew.

And he'd say

"It's because he sucked! He didn't blow, he sucked! And it's really hard to blow a house of bricks down, but I'll tell you summat …"

and we all had to go

"What, Granddad?"

and he would say

"It's impossible to suck a house down! It's impossible because once you start sucking your false teeth get dislodged and you accidentally suck 'em down your throat!'

and we'd have to go

"Oh no, Granddad!"

And then he'd open his mouth wide and we'd have to look at the scars at the back of his throat from when he sucked in his false teeth by accident on that boat just off Whitby …

Polly Put Your Flat Cap On

Polly put your flat cap on
Polly put your flat cap on
Polly put your flat cap on
We'll all have a laugh!

Polly it is far too tight
Polly it is far too tight
Polly it is far too tight
Your face is blue!

Polly let us pull and pull
Polly let us pull and pull
Polly let us pull and pull
It won't come off!

POLLY PUT YOUR FLAT CAP ON

Polly let's try oil and grease
Polly let's try oil and grease
Polly let's try oil and grease
It just won't budge!

Polly it will have to stay
Polly it will have to stay
Polly it will have to stay
It won't come off!

Polly can you hear me love?
Polly can you hear me love?
Polly can you hear me love?
You're
Very
Blue!

T' Invisible Man of Methley

They seek him here, they seek him theer, they seek him every Methley-wheer, that Jack o' t' Hedge, that Will o' t' wisp, that no-bloke, that cap-hung-on-nowt, that see-through chap, that empty glass, that breeze ruffling yer muffler, that hole in the street.

They seek him here, they seek him theer, they seek him every Methley-wheer, that absent kid in t' schoolroom, that free seat at t' evening scran, that shadder by t' winder that's not a shadder o' nothin' at all.

They seek him here, they seek him theer, they seek him every Methley-wheer, that rustlin' o' t' curtains in a cold parlour, that throat cleared in an attic where nobody's ivver

bin, that sprite, that elf, that boggart, that what-the-ummer.

They should hev looked i' mi shed. Ah've gorrim. Ah feed 'im bacon.

(from Yorksheer Legends,
Methley Monthly Publications, 1912)

Two Yorkshiremen
Argue Over the Title
of a Half-Forgotten Fairy Tale

Seth: Ah'm tellin thi, it were 'Goldilocks and t' Three Beers'. She has a good neet art.

Jed: Ah'm tellin thi, it were Goldilocks and t' Three Stairs'. She converts a bungalow unambitiously.

Seth: Ah'm tellin thi, it were 'Goldilocks and t' Three Hairs'. She has a combover.

Jed: Ah'm tellin thi, it were 'Goldilocks and t' Three Hares'. She thinks they're rabbits.

Seth: Ah'm tellin thi, it were 'Goldilocks and t' Three Heirs'. They're all fake princes an' all.

Jed: Ah'm tellin thi, it were 'Goldilocks and t' Three Chairs'. It were set in a furniture shop.

Seth: Ah'm tellin thi, it were 'Goldilocks and t' Three Players'. It were about that football team that had a lot sent off.

Jed: Ah'm tellin thi, it were 'Goldilocks and t' Three Layers'. She eyts a big cake.

(There's room here to invent your own, gentle reader…)

T' Apostrophe Eater o' t' Dales

One day the folks of Swaledale got up and noticed that all the apostrophes had disappeared from their speech.

So, instead of saying "I'm going up t' dale to t' shops and t' pub" they ended up saying "I'm going up dale to shops and pub" which may not seem, to outsiders, like much of a difference but can in fact render older speakers breathless and younger speakers confused.

The folks of Swaledale sent for T' Apostrophe Police who arrived hot-foot from t' office in Leyburn. They investigated missing apostrophes and came to a terrible conclusion: T' Apostrophe Eater, long thought to be extinct, had reared its ugly head and was once

more on t' loose eating all t' apostrophes it could find.

T' Apostrophe Police went out into the wilder end of Swaledale with T' Apostrophe Eater Gun and T' Apostrophe Eater Net. They stood and listened … in a cottage at the end of a rutted track they could hear the sound of munching and someone shouting

"Hes got me apostrophes and I cant be a proper Yorkshireman no more!"

T'Apostrophe Police ran down the rutted track with T' Gun and T' Net, and a terrible sight met their eyes.

There it was: T'Apostrophe Eater, gobbling up all t' apostrophes poor old farmer Wilks was uttering as fast as he could speak them, like they were flies, like a blob of t' dung of a hoss. T' Apostrophe Marksman fired off several rounds of T' Apostrophe Gun but, in his haste, he had it back to front. And you can guess what ha'ppened n'ext...

S'o now that par't of Sw'ale'dale is know'n as apo'strophe dal'e. An'd t'apo'strophe ea'te'r i's sti'l'l ou't the're so'm'e'wh'e're...

'Oranges and Lemons'
the original, Yorkshire, version

I like my parkin
Say the bells of St Martin

I'm never full
Say the big bells of Hull

I like to eat faster
Say the bells of Tadcaster

Give me that pork
Says the great bell of York

Curd tart is for me
Say the bells of Whitby

My false teeth hate seeds
Say the bells of old Leeds

My tea must be strong
Says the fat bell of Tong

Here comes a bread knife
To cut up your crusts
— Don't you dare touch 'em!
To
Eat
Them's
A
Must!

Yorkshire Fairy Tales
Unknown Except for Their Titles

The Little Stick Seller
and the Thoughtful Duck

The Happiness Clog
and the Unhappy Slipper

Prince Frank of Halifax's Throne of Parkin

The Little Boy Who Found The Coal
that Turned Everything into Gold
and Then Lost it on The Bus to Ripon

The Talking Fish Who Wanted to Shut Up

A Smile is Worth More than A Frown
Except on Tuesdays in Northallerton

DAFT YORKSHIRE FAIRY TALES

Simple Simon's Brother Jed

The Snow Queen
and the One-Bar Electric Fire

The Cat, The Dog, The Horse, The Rat,
The Sheep, The Hedgehog, The Badger,
The Trout, The Toad, The Newt, The Gerbil
who all Did Nothing of Note Ever

The Crown of Sausage

The Bells That Wouldn't Stop Chiming
or
Give Them Here, I'll Stop the Flipping Things

Bill's Mirror That Always Showed
Huddersfield Wherever You Were When You
Looked Into It

Thistle Pie For Tea

Gold, E-Locks, Hand The Three, Bares
(This last one may have been transcribed wrongly.)

And they all lived happily ever after.
And as each year went by
*   they all got much dafter*
With each passing decade
*   the sound of their laughter*
Reached from the parlour
*   straight up to the rafters*
They had laughing for starters
*   and laughing for afters*
They worked hard at laughing,
*   they were laughter grafters*

So they obviously weren't from Yorkshire